Ava and Jayden were right, weren't they? This piece does sound like a bird flying higher and higher. It was composed by Ralph Vaughan Williams. The violin is perfect for pretending to be a bird, because it can soar really high and flutter, like a bird flapping its wings. Ralph was inspired partly by a poem about a lark.

Can you guess how many parts a violin has? The answer is 70! Some of them have funny names. The rounded part at the top is called a "scroll," and the piece of wood the strings sit on is called a "bridge," although you can't walk over it.

One click, and oh my – you will hear the lark fly!

The most famous violin maker came from Italy and was called Stradivari. People love Stradivarius violins so much that they pay millions of pounds for them.

Someone who makes or repairs violins is called a luthier.

Ava and Jayden are enjoying a picnic in a clearing in the woods. A shaft of golden sunshine bathes everything in a warm glow and picks out a swan gliding serenely on the water. "What a beautiful bird," Jayden says, pointing. "It's moving so slowly and gracefully."

Ava and Jayden start to dance, copying the swan's movements. As they do, a cello begins to play. The cello has four strings and is played with a bow, but it is much bigger than a violin. Suddenly, the swan flaps its huge wings and takes off into the sky.

Cellos

The cello is the only instrument in the orchestra that the player wraps their legs around!

In this piece of music, the smooth cello is the swan, and the piano sounds like the water rippling underneath the bird as it swims. Did you notice how serene it sounds? The swan is one of many animals made into music by Camille Saint-Saëns. He also made donkeys, hens, lions, and even an elephant into music, too.

Say hello to the cello! It is made of wood. You must agree, it sounds very good.

Give this a press. What happens? Can you guess?

A clarinet is made of five pieces, all black.
It comes in a case for you to unpack.

The bustling city is filled with tall, shiny buildings that stretch far up into the sky. "Look at all the different shapes!" Jayden says. "That one is shaped like a pencil," Ava replies.

Ava and Jayden wander down the street. A man on the corner is starting a tune on his clarinet. A clarinet is a tube-shaped wooden instrument that you blow into. It has holes and silver keys. The city noises sound like musical instruments, too. "Could the sounds of the city have inspired music like the sounds of nature have?" wonders Jayden.

Clarinets

This amazing sound was made by a clarinet playing as part of an orchestra. George Gershwin wrote this piece. He loved jazz music, which originated in America – his home country. Gershwin wrote a lot of music for Broadway shows. Broadway is the famous theatre area of New York City.

The clarinet has a family of instruments. They range from the tiny "piccolo" clarinet to the huge "contrabass" clarinet. It has a three-metre-long tube and makes a very deep sound!

It's here that you click for the ebony stick!

Out in the countryside, Ava and Jayden are visiting a beehive. "Bees are such clever things," says Ava. "Did you know they're vital for our plants?" Jayden nods. "They make honey for my toast, too," he says. "Yum!"

A nearby musician starts playing a melody on a flute. She blows over its hole and presses little buttons called keys with her fingers. It sounds like a bee buzzing quickly from flower to flower.

Ava and Jayden watch the bees at work until suddenly, they all rise into the air and buzz away. As the bees disappear, so does the flute music.

The shiny flute goes toot, toot, toot. Some people play it in a suit.

Flutes

The flute was pretending to be a bumblebee in that music. It moved fast and seemed to be fluttering, just like a bee's wings. Nikolai Rimsky-Korsakov wrote the music as part of an opera, which is a big story set to music. Can you sing as many notes as the flute can? Does your voice go as high as a flute?

Give the button a push. Then simply ...shush!

The flute is the only instrument in the orchestra that is held sideways to be played. There are left-handed and right-handed versions. Someone who plays a flute is called a flautist.

Outside, snow is falling. Ava and Jayden are in an old, grand room watching a ballet class. There are rails around the walls and a shiny wooden floor. "And... plié, two, three..." calls the teacher. "A plié is a knee bend," says Jayden. "I know because I go to lessons. Try it, Ava."

The teacher is dancing like a swan. "My arms are like wings, and my chest is puffed out," she says. She is dancing to music played on an instrument called an oboe. The oboe player looks like he is blowing up a giant balloon!

Two reeds bound together as one poke out of the top of the oboe. When the player blows the instrument, the reeds vibrate to make a sound. Reeds must be carefully carved before they are used.

The oboe has no strings to pluck.
Some say it can sound like a duck.

Oboes

Doesn't the oboe sound beautiful? It is playing music from *Swan Lake*, a ballet by Peter Tchaikovsky. It tells the story of Odette, a princess turned into a swan by a magic spell.

press the button – go on – to hear a fine swan.

It's summer, and Ava and Jayden are on the slopes of an alpine mountain. They can see a man playing a curly, whirly instrument made out of shiny brass. It's called a French horn.

Jayden nudges Ava. "How long do you think the curly part of that horn would stretch if it was unraveled?" he asks. Ava is proud that she knows the answer. "Nearly four metres," she says.

"I like your costume, Jayden," says Ava. Jayden is dressed as Wolfgang Amadeus Mozart, a famous composer from the 1700s. "Mozart was born somewhere like this," Jayden explains. "So I wanted to look like him. I might even keep it on for the concert we're going to later!"

Horn players are the only players to stick their hand down the open end of their instrument while they are playing it. Doing that allows them to change the note.

The horn sounds very soft and kind. It's curly, and it points behind.

French horns

That was music written for the French horn by a man named Wolfgang Amadeus Mozart. Isn't it fun? The horn sounds velvety and smooth, even though it is playing quite fast. Did it make you feel all warm and happy?

Give this a press for some French horn finesse.

Mozart wrote this and other horn pieces for his good friend Joseph. Mozart would sometimes write the music in different colours to make his friend laugh.

Jayden and Ava are exploring backstage at an opera house. "Look at all this stuff!" says Jayden. There are thick ropes, levers, bright lights, and a trapdoor that lets people appear suddenly on stage, as if by magic.

Suddenly, something makes Jayden jump. "What's that?!" he shouts. Ava looks more closely. "Don't worry, Jayden. It's just people practising for the performance." There are five actors dressed as knights on horses, and one of them is blowing a gold-coloured instrument. "That's a trumpet," Jayden explains. "They can make really loud sounds. Imagine trying to play its three valves while holding onto the horse's reins and not falling off!"

If you stand next to a trumpet, it's loud – so just lump it.

The valves of the trumpet are the buttons that stick out at the top. The trumpet has only three valves, but it can play more than 30 different notes.

Trumpets

Wow! That got your attention, didn't it? It was music played by the trumpets in an orchestra. Trumpets often play loud music. This piece was written for an opera by an Italian composer called Gioachino Rossini. Do you think it sounds like the trumpets are calling people?

Press the button round to hear the trumpet sound!

Jayden and Ava find themselves aboard a special type of boat called a barge, and it has a piano on top. They're looking at all the different types of houses painted in many bright colours.

"How many windows can you count, Jayden?" asks Ava. "I'll count in a minute," he replies. "I'm just listening to the music." Through the open windows of the houses, they can see people practising their pianos. Jayden is entranced. "The piano is different from the other instruments we've heard. It can play a lot of notes at once," he says.

Black and white keys are really great.
Count them – there are 88.

Piano

You've just heard a piece of piano music composed by a woman named Clara Schumann. The piano was playing loudly with an orchestra. Which direction did the piano go: up or down? The piano is lucky because, unlike many other instruments, it can play a lot of notes at once – just as long as you have enough fingers to play them.

The piano's full name is the pianoforte, which means quiet/loud in Italian. Before it was called this, it was called the fortepiano – which means loud/quiet! Maybe they couldn't make their minds up?!

Clara Schumann started writing this piece of music when she was only 13. By the time she was 16, it was finished, and she played it at a concert conducted by the great composer Felix Mendelssohn.

Click firmly on this bright round key for do re mi!

The sun is just coming up when Ava and Jayden arrive at a mysterious rock formation. "It's beautiful," Ava says, staring.

Jayden picks up a stick and starts to tap it on a rock. "1, 2, 3, 4... 1, 2, 3, 4..." he counts. Ava joins in but is careful to tap her stick only when Jayden says "2" and "4." They keep tapping louder and louder, until Jayden's stick snaps. Oops!

"Hitting stones must've been the first way people learned to make musical sounds. I just hope they had stronger sticks!" laughs Jayden.

The largest timpani drum ever made was nearly two metres wide. If you measured the circle of the drum's skin, it would be 1.7 metres around.

Timpani

Listen to that music! After the opening notes, the timpani player bangs the drums powerfully. They go from one drum to the other and back again, over and over. Have you ever played a drum? The timpani drum player uses beaters to hit the drums. This part of the music is all about a sunrise. When does the sun rise?

Another name for a timpani drum is kettledrum — because the drums are made using copper, just like an old-style kettle. The difference between a kettledrum and a kettle is that a kettle is used to make tea, while a kettledrum can only play "ti."

If you ever feel sad and glum, just smile – and beat loud on a drum.

Press a finger or thumb... for the sound of a drum!

Jayden and Ava's last stop on their magical musical adventure is the River Thames in London. They're just in time for a grand procession on the water.

The boat at the front is coloured red and gold and is very, very grand. "Who's on that one?" asks Jayden. "That's the Queen's boat," replies Ava. "It has her coat of arms engraved on the side."

The crowd starts to sing a song to celebrate the Queen. They all sing different notes that fit together – it's called harmony. Ava and Jayden join in. "I want to go on a musical adventure every day," says Ava. "Me too!" agrees Jayden.

Some sing low. Some sing higher.
Some sing with friends in a choir.

Choir

When you sing, the sound comes out of your mouth at around 1,200 km per hour. That's three times faster than the fastest ever train!

Let's all rejoice... press the button to hear the voice!

You've just heard music by a composer called George Frideric Handel sung to the word "Hallelujah." Did it sound happy or sad to you? It's a chorus that comes from a piece of music for many singers. How many people do you think were singing? "Hallelujah" is an old word used to express joy or thanks.

Celebratory songs are some of the best-known songs. "Happy Birthday to You" appears in the Guinness World Records as the most recognized song in the English language. What songs do you like to sing?

Here we can see all the members of an orchestra together. Have you noticed that there are more string players than anything else? This is because they are not as loud as other instruments and so more of them are needed. Can you spot the instruments mentioned in this book? There are other instruments too: a bassoon, a tuba, and a double bass. There is also the person at the front who directs the orchestra using a baton. They are the conductor, and their job is to make sure that all of the instruments are played at the right time.

The orchestra

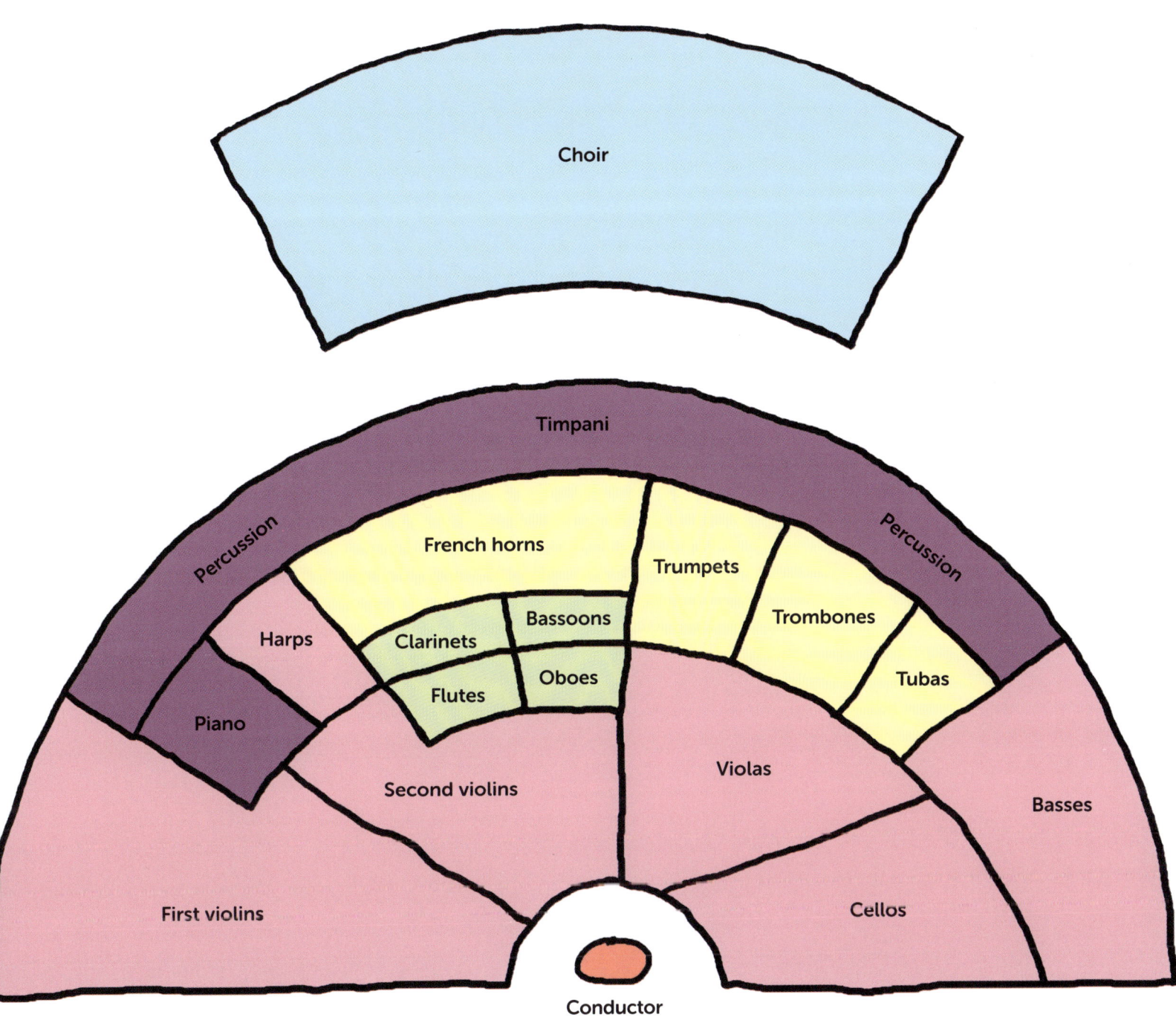

As you've read this book, you'll have noticed that every instrument in the orchestra has its place. There are four sections: strings (pink), woodwinds (green), brass (yellow), and percussion (purple). Here you can look down on the orchestra and see how all the sections fit together. Which section would you like to be part of? Some instruments move around depending on the piece of music. For example, the piano moves to the front if it has a solo but is at the back if it is part of the full orchestra.

Meet the composers

George Gershwin

George Gershwin (1898–1937) was born in Brooklyn, New York. He wrote the music for a lot of songs, with his brother, Ira, writing the words. One of them was called "I'm a Poached Egg." It was a love song.

Ralph Vaughan Williams

Ralph Vaughan Williams (1872–1958) was born in England. He loved the folk songs of the United Kingdom, so he went with friends around the country asking people to sing them to him so he could write them down. Some of the songs we still sing today were collected by him.

Nikolai Rimsky-Korsakov

Nikolai Rimsky-Korsakov (1844–1908) was born in Russia. He was torn between being a sailor, like his older brother, or devoting himself to music. As a young boy, he would read book after book about the sea, and his love of the sea even influenced his music.

Peter Ilyich Tchaikovsky

Peter Ilyich Tchaikovsky (1840–1893) was born in west Russia. He composed the music for three ballets: *Swan Lake*, *Sleeping Beauty,* and *The Nutcracker*.

Camille Saint-Saëns

Camille Saint-Saëns (1835–1921) was born more than 100 years ago in Paris, France. He wanted only his close friends to hear the music he composed. He refused to let anyone put it in a book for others to read and play.

Clara Schumann

Clara Schumann (1819–1896) was born in Germany. She was one of the first concert pianists to play completely from memory without the music in front of her.

Gioachino Rossini

Gioachino Rossini (1792–1868) was born in Italy. Not only was he a great composer, but he was also a pretty good cook. He had a lot of recipes named after him, including "Chicken Rossini" and even "Poached Eggs Rossini." Delizioso!

Wolfgang Amadeus Mozart

Wolfgang Amadeus Mozart (1756–1791) was born in Austria. He is probably the most well-known of all the group often called "The Great Composers" – they are like the superheroes of music. Mozart's superpower was that he could compose in his head, then write out a totally finished piece of music as if he were simply downloading it. He also had great first names: Johannes Chrysostomus Wolfgangus Theophilus... Mozart.

Richard Strauss

Richard Strauss (1864–1949) was born in Munich, Germany. He had already composed hundreds of pieces of music before he even left school. He loved to play a game with friends called Skat, which is a three-handed card game. Strauss, himself, had only two hands.

George Frideric Handel

George Frideric Handel (1685–1759) was born in Brandenburg-Prussia, which is now part of Germany. His father didn't want him to be a musician, so he had to have a keyboard smuggled up to the attic and kept hidden. He would play it in the middle of the night so that he wouldn't be found out.

Legendary performers

Cello

American YO-YO MA is one of the world's most famous cello players. He performed at Carnegie Hall in New York City when he was just nine years old! SHEKU KANNEH-MASON is a popular British cello player. He played at the Duke and Duchess of Sussex's wedding.

Violin

One of the world's greatest violinists is NICOLA BENEDETTI from Scotland. She plays on a Stradivarius violin that has been loaned to her, and it is worth more than £6 million! JOSHUA BELL is from the US, and he has performed in front of Michelle Obama at the White House.

Oboe

ALBRECHT MAYER is a German oboist. He likes to perform music that was not composed for the oboe but was instead meant to be sung.

Clarinet

MARTIN FRÖST is a clarinet player from Sweden who is often very lively when he is playing. German clarinetist SABINE MEYER was one of the first women to be part of the Berlin Philharmonic orchestra. She now plays as a soloist.

Flute

One of the most famous flautists in the world comes from Belfast in Northern Ireland. His name is JAMES GALWAY, although some people call him "The Man with the Golden Flute." He does, in fact, own an 18-carat gold flute!

French Horn

FELIX KLIESER is an incredible horn player from Germany. He was born without arms and so plays with his feet. DENNIS BRAIN was one of the most famous British horn players. His party trick was to play the horn with a length of garden hose. He would cut lengths off to tune to different notes.

Timpani

The world's most famous percussionist is DAME EVELYN GLENNIE. She was born in Scotland and has been profoundly deaf since she was 12. She hears music in different ways, such as through vibrations and feel.

Trumpet

WYNTON MARSALIS is a great trumpet player from the US who can play jazz music as well as classical music. ALISON BALSOM from England is a world-famous trumpet player, but she also has a talent for woodworking and furniture making.

Piano

The Chinese pianist LANG LANG was inspired to learn to play the piano while watching *Tom and Jerry* cartoons when he was just two years old. Argentinian MARTHA ARGERICH has been called the greatest living pianist. She performed her first full concert when she was only eight years old. She's now 80 and is still performing to huge audiences.

Voice

LUCIANO PAVAROTTI was a great Italian singer who was known around the world. When he left school, he had to choose between singing and becoming a professional footballer. He chose scores over scoring! Today, a lot of people like to sing together in choirs. THE SIXTEEN CHOIR from England is made up of... guess how many people?

Did you spot the earworm?

In music, earworms are songs that you just can't get out of your head. Did you spot Ernie the earworm hiding on the pages of this book? If so, well done! If you didn't, why not look again now – there are 11 earworms to find.

Answers: **p. 3** In the auditorium seats. **p. 5** Behind the teapot. **p. 7** In the front seat of the green van. **p. 8** Behind the leaf. **p. 11** On the window ledge. **p. 13** In the flowers. **p. 14** On top of the lights. **p. 16** In the window of the orange building. **p. 18** Next to the rock. **p. 21** In the crowd. **p. 22** Playing the triangle.

Acknowledgements

Published by Dorling Kindersley Ltd in association with Classic FM, part of Global Media and Entertainment Group Ltd.

All music licensed by courtesy of Naxos Music UK Limited.

"The Lark Ascending" by Ralph Vaughan Williams copyright © Oxford University Press 1925. All rights reserved.

Sounds edited by James Brady

Text copyright © Tim Lihoreau and Philip Noyce, 2022

Artwork copyright © Olga Baumert, 2022

DK | Penguin Random House

Editor Vicky Armstrong
Senior Designer Clive Savage
Production Editor Siu Yin Chan
Senior Production Controller Louise Daly
Senior Acquisitions Editor Katy Flint
Managing Art Editor Vicky Short
Publishing Director Mark Searle

First published in Great Britain in 2022 by
Dorling Kindersley Limited
DK, One Embassy Gardens, 8 Viaduct Gardens,
London SW11 7BW

The authorised representative in the EEA is Dorling Kindersley Verlag GmbH. Arnulfstr. 124, 80636 Munich, Germany.
Copyright © 2022 Dorling Kindersley Limited
A Penguin Random House Company

10 9 8 7 6 5 4 3 2

003–329055–Sep/22

Printed and bound in China

For the curious

www.dk.com